You Are Being Watched

Digital Privacy Uncovered

By Synthia Vance

1st Edition

Copyright © 2025 Marc M. Paper Company

From the author

When I first began grappling with the role of technology in my life, it wasn't a grand revelation but a series of small, nagging moments. I'd find myself scrolling mindlessly through social media at night, wondering where my evening had gone.

My smartwatch would buzz constantly, even during moments I had set aside to focus or unwind. My phone, a tool meant to connect and inform me, felt more like a leash, tethering me to a cycle of endless notifications. I realized I wasn't using technology, it was using me.

I wasn't alone in this struggle. Friends and colleagues voiced similar frustrations: the creeping anxiety of never truly being "off," the pressure to curate perfect online personas, the nagging guilt of spending too much time online yet feeling disconnected. It wasn't that we hated technology, far from it. We loved the convenience, the innovation, and the way it brought people and ideas into our lives. But we were stuck in a constant tug-of-war between the benefits and the drawbacks.

My breaking point came during what should have been a relaxing family dinner. My young daughter was telling me about her day at school, and instead of giving her my full attention, I glanced at my phone to check an email notification. Her face fell, and she quietly stopped speaking. I put the phone down immediately, but the damage was done. That moment made me realize I needed to take a hard look at how technology was shaping not just my life, but my relationships and my priorities.

I started diving into books, articles, and research papers to understand the role of technology in modern life. I read about productivity tools, digital detoxes, and even the ethical dilemmas of AI and data privacy. I learned how technology could enhance our minds, bodies, and emotional well-being, but also how it could undermine us if we weren't careful. Despite all the valuable information out there, I noticed a glaring gap: there wasn't a single comprehensive resource that tied all these aspects together. Each topic was treated as an isolated concern, but no one was addressing how these issues intersected to form the bigger picture of our "digital selves."

I realized I wasn't just struggling with time management or social media habits, I was grappling with my 'Techno(logy)self'. Technology wasn't just a set of tools, it was an extension of my identity. How I used, or misused, it affected my cognitive clarity, physical health, emotional balance, and even my ethics. What I wanted wasn't just a how-to guide for digital life. I wanted a roadmap for using technology in a way that aligned with my values and aspirations.

That's when the idea for this book took root. If I was struggling to navigate this complex relationship with technology, surely others were too. I wanted to create something practical yet reflective, actionable yet deeply personal. A book that not only helped readers address specific challenges, like reducing screen time or enhancing productivity, but also invited them to rethink their overall relationship with technology.

Throughout the process of writing this book, I've tested and refined every strategy and insight shared here. I've experienced the ups and downs of building my Technoself, from the triumph of finally sticking to a digital detox to the frustration of slipping back into old habits. This journey has been humbling and transformative, and it's my hope that this book will serve as a guide for anyone navigating similar struggles.

Ultimately, this book isn't just about technology, it's about empowerment. It's about taking control of how technology shapes your life, instead of letting it control you. It's about rediscovering the power of intentionality and balance, so you can use technology to enhance your mind, body, and spirit. If you've ever felt overwhelmed by the digital age, this book was written for you.

Let's navigate this journey together.

Synthia

Contents

Understanding Digital Privacy

Digital privacy is a myth. That may sound like an exaggeration, but consider this: every click, every search, and every purchase you make online is recorded, analysed, and often sold. The promise of privacy in the digital age is often no more than an illusion, carefully crafted to make us feel safe while our data is mined for profit. If you think you're not being watched, think again. The reality is, whether you're scrolling through social media, using GPS to navigate, or just browsing the web, someone, somewhere, is collecting your information.

The question isn't whether your data is being collected, it's how much of it is being collected and who's using it. What's worse, the sheer scale of this data collection is something most of us don't fully grasp. For many, privacy feels like a right, a given. But in today's hyperconnected world, it's less of a right and more of a privilege, one that requires constant effort to maintain.

But what exactly is digital privacy? Simply put, it refers to the right to control your personal information online. It's the ability to decide who has access to your data, how it is used, and whether it remains secure. In an ideal world, digital privacy would be as natural as locking the door to your home. Unfortunately, the digital landscape is far from secure. Many companies, governments, and even hackers actively seek to access, exploit, or monitor our personal data.

Digital privacy matters for many reasons. It's not just about keeping your passwords safe or avoiding annoying ads. It's about safeguarding your freedom to express yourself without fear, ensuring your personal safety, and preserving your right to make choices about your own life. Without privacy, everything from your location to your preferences and even your deepest thoughts could be up for grabs. And as history has shown, a lack of privacy can have serious consequences.

To truly appreciate the importance of digital privacy, it helps to understand how we got here. Just a few decades ago, most of our personal lives were off-limits to the outside world. Letters were private, phone conversations were difficult to tap, and personal details weren't shared so freely. But with the advent of the internet, smartphones, and social media, this has changed dramatically. Today, the lines between public and private life are blurred, and protecting your privacy has become a more complex task.

The advent of artificial intelligence and big data has further complicated matters. AI systems can analyse massive datasets to draw conclusions about individuals, even from seemingly innocuous information. For example, machine learning algorithms can predict your political preferences, health conditions, and even future behaviours based on your online activities. This level of surveillance and prediction raises critical questions about consent and control.

In this chapter, we'll dive into the foundational concepts of digital privacy. We'll explore how personal data is collected, stored, and shared. We'll also take a closer look at the key players involved: tech companies, advertisers, governments, and even cybercriminals. By understanding these forces, you can take the first step toward protecting yourself in the digital age.

So why does this matter to you? Because every time you browse the web, post on social media, or shop online, you're leaving behind a trail of information that can be used in ways you might not expect. This chapter is your guide to understanding what's at stake and why you should care. Let's begin by defining what digital privacy really means and why it's crucial for everyone in today's world. These forces, you can take the first step toward protecting yourself in the digital age.

So why does this matter to you? Because every time you browse the web, post on social media, or shop online, you're leaving behind a trail of information that can be used in ways you might not expect. This chapter is your guide to understanding what's at stake and why you should care. Let's begin by defining what digital privacy really means and why it's crucial for everyone in today's world.

What is Digital Privacy?

Digital privacy is the right to control your personal information and how it is used online. It encompasses everything from the data you share on social media to the search history you generate while browsing. At its core, digital privacy is about choice: the choice to decide who can see your data, how it is used, and whether it remains secure.

For instance, when you log into a website and provide your email address, you are sharing personal information. If that website sells your email to advertisers, your privacy has been compromised. Similarly, when you search for a product online, you may notice ads for that product following you across different websites. This happens because your browsing behaviour has been tracked, and your data has been shared with advertisers.

The concept of digital privacy is relatively new, but it has become a cornerstone of our digital lives. It's not just a technical issue for IT experts to solve; it's a human right that affects everyone. Whether you're a student, a professional, or a retiree, your data has value, and protecting it is crucial.

Digital privacy also extends to metadata, the data about data. For example, when you send an email, the metadata includes details like the time it was sent, the recipient, and the device used. Even without the email's content, this metadata can reveal a lot about your habits and connections. This makes metadata a valuable resource for companies and governments alike.

How Did We Get Here?
A Brief History of Digital Privacy

The journey to today's digital privacy landscape began with the internet's rise in the late 20th century. Before the internet, privacy was easier to manage. Most communication was analog, and personal information wasn't as easily accessible. But as technology advanced, so did the methods for collecting and sharing data.

In the early days of the internet, privacy was not a major concern. Websites collected minimal information, and users were mostly anonymous. However, the rise of search engines, social media platforms, and e-commerce changed the game. Companies like Google and Amazon realized that data was valuable. They started collecting information about user behaviour to improve their services and, more importantly, to sell targeted ads.

The introduction of smartphones added another layer to this equation. With mobile apps tracking everything from your location to your health data, the amount of personal information being collected skyrocketed. Social media platforms like Facebook encouraged users to share every aspect of their lives, making personal data a commodity. Today, data collection is so pervasive that even seemingly harmless actions, like liking a post or clicking on a link, contribute to your digital profile.

This shift also brought about the concept of the "surveillance economy," where the primary currency is data. Companies began to offer free services, like email, social media, and search engines, in exchange for access to user data. While these services made life more convenient, they came at the cost of privacy. Users unknowingly became the product, with their data being sold to advertisers and other third parties.

The emergence of artificial intelligence further amplified these trends. AI systems can analyse vast amounts of data to identify patterns, predict behaviours, and even manipulate decisions. For instance, personalized content recommendations on platforms like YouTube or Netflix are powered by AI algorithms that learn from your viewing history. While convenient, these systems also raise questions about privacy and control.

How Personal Data is Collected, Stored, and Shared

Every time you use the internet, you leave behind a digital footprint. Here's how it works:

1. **Collection:** Your data is collected through various means, including cookies, web forms, and app

permissions. For example, when you download an app, it might ask for access to your contacts, location, and photos. Even if you're not actively sharing this information, it can still be collected passively through tracking technologies.

Beyond cookies and apps, your data is also collected through "smart" devices like fitness trackers, smartwatches, and even connected home appliances. These devices continuously gather information about your habits, health, and environment.

2. **Storage:** Once collected, your data is stored in databases, often referred to as data warehouses. These can belong to companies, governments, or even third-party data brokers. Some companies store your data indefinitely, while others may delete it after a certain period.

   Data storage also raises concerns about security. Hackers often target databases to steal sensitive information, leading to data breaches that can have far-reaching consequences for individuals and organizations.

3. **Sharing:** Data sharing happens behind the scenes, often without your explicit consent. For example, a shopping website might share your email address

with advertisers, or a social media platform might sell your browsing behaviour to analytics firms. In some cases, your data can even be accessed by law enforcement agencies or hackers.

One lesser-known aspect of data sharing is "data enrichment," where multiple data sources are combined to create a more detailed profile of an individual. This practice is commonly used by advertisers to target specific demographics.

The Main Actors in Digital Privacy

When we talk about digital privacy, it's important to recognize the key players involved. These actors have varying motivations and impacts on our personal data. Some work to exploit it for profit, others aim to protect it, and a few operate in Gray areas. Understanding these groups is essential to grasp the broader digital privacy landscape.

Tech companies are among the most influential players in this space. They've built vast ecosystems that thrive on user data, offering free services like social media platforms, search engines, and apps in exchange for personal information. Companies like Google and Facebook have created business models cantered around collecting, analysing, and monetizing data. On the surface, these services make life easier, you get personalized recommendations, convenient features, and access to global networks. However, the trade-off is your privacy.

Advertisers and data brokers also play a significant role. Advertisers rely on targeted marketing to maximize their impact, and data brokers supply them with the detailed profiles they need. These brokers aggregate data from various sources, including social media activity, purchase history, and even public records. The result? Highly personalized ads that seem to "know" what you're thinking.

Governments and law enforcement agencies enter the picture with a different agenda. They justify data collection as a means to ensure national security, prevent crime, or improve public services. However, this often comes at the cost of individual freedoms. Surveillance programs, such as those revealed by Edward Snowden, show how far-reaching and intrusive these practices can be.

Finally, we cannot ignore cybercriminals and hackers. Unlike the actors mentioned earlier, their goals are purely malicious. They exploit vulnerabilities in digital systems to steal data, commit fraud, or disrupt services. Their actions highlight the importance of robust cybersecurity measures to protect personal information from falling into the wrong hands.

But who are these players?

Tech Companies: Giants like Google, Facebook, and Amazon thrive on data. They collect, analyse, and monetize user data to fuel their business models. For example, Google uses your search history to deliver personalized ads, while Amazon tracks your purchases to recommend products. These companies often justify their data collection practices by claiming they improve user experience.

Advertisers and Data Brokers: These players buy and sell your data to target ads more effectively. Data brokers aggregate information from multiple sources, creating detailed profiles that can include everything from your income level to your favourite hobbies. Companies like Acxiom and Experian specialize in this type of data aggregation.

Governments and Law Enforcement Agencies: Governments collect data for various reasons, including national security and law enforcement. However, this often comes at the cost of individual privacy. Surveillance programs like those revealed by Edward Snowden show how governments can monitor citizens on a massive scale. Even democratic nations have implemented laws that allow for extensive data collection, such as the Patriot Act in the United States.

Cybercriminals and Hackers: Not all threats come from legitimate entities. Hackers and cybercriminals seek to exploit your data for financial gain. This can include stealing credit card numbers, hacking email accounts, or even engaging in identity theft. Ransomware attacks, where hackers encrypt data and demand payment for its release, have also become increasingly common.

AI and Algorithm Developers: While not a traditional actor, the developers of AI systems play a crucial role in shaping the digital privacy landscape. Their algorithms decide what data is collected, how it is analysed, and what insights are derived. These decisions can have significant implications for privacy, often without users even realizing it.

Why Digital Privacy Matters

Digital privacy is not just a matter of preference; it's a fundamental right. It underpins our ability to live freely, make decisions, and engage with the world without fear of intrusion. The erosion of privacy affects everyone, regardless of their level of technical knowledge or online activity.

Imagine living in a world where every action is monitored and judged. Without privacy, you might hesitate to research sensitive topics, voice dissenting opinions, or even explore new interests. This chilling effect stifles creativity, limits self-expression, and undermines democracy. Privacy allows us to think, learn, and communicate without undue influence or fear.

The issue extends beyond freedom of expression. Digital privacy also plays a critical role in personal safety. From identity theft to online harassment, the misuse of personal data can lead to real-world harm. For instance, exposing someone's location or financial details can make them vulnerable to fraud, stalking, or worse. By safeguarding privacy, we reduce these risks and create a safer digital environment.

Moreover, privacy ensures autonomy. In a data-driven world, our choices are increasingly shaped by algorithms that use personal information to predict and influence behaviour. This might seem convenient at first, after all, who doesn't like personalized recommendations? But it also means losing control over your own decisions. Without privacy, you're at the mercy of systems designed to prioritize profit over your well-being.

Finally, digital privacy is essential for building trust. Whether it's between individuals, businesses, or governments, trust is the foundation of any healthy relationship. When organizations respect privacy, they foster loyalty and confidence among their users. Conversely, breaches of trust, like unauthorized data collection or security lapses, damage reputations and erode confidence.

Protecting digital privacy is about more than avoiding inconvenience or embarrassment. It's about preserving the fundamental rights and freedoms that allow us to thrive in a connected world. As we explore the complexities of this issue, remember that privacy is not a luxury, it's a necessity.

To recap the key points here on why digital privacy matters:

Freedom of Expression: Without privacy, people may hesitate to express their opinions or share sensitive information. This can stifle free speech and creativity.

Personal Safety: A lack of privacy can lead to serious consequences, such as identity theft, stalking, or harassment. Protecting your data helps safeguard your personal safety.

Control Over Your Life: Your data reflects who you are. Losing control over it can lead to decisions being made about you without your input, such as being denied a loan or being targeted with misleading ads.

Preventing Exploitation: Companies and governments can exploit your data in ways that benefit them but harm you. By protecting your privacy, you can minimize the risk of exploitation.

Building Trust: Digital privacy fosters trust between individuals and organizations. When companies prioritize privacy, they are more likely to earn the trust and loyalty of their users.

Conclusion

Understanding digital privacy is the first step toward protecting yourself in a world where data is currency. By knowing what digital privacy is, how it's compromised, and why it matters, you can take proactive steps to safeguard your information. In the chapters ahead, we'll explore specific aspects of digital privacy, from the role of tech companies to the tools you can use to stay anonymous. Remember, your data is valuable, treat it like the treasure it is.

Surveillance Capitalism: The Economy of Data

Imagine walking into a store where the salesperson knows not only what you're looking for, but also what you've bought in the past, your favourite colours, your budget, and even what you're likely to buy next. Sounds convenient, right? But what if this salesperson wasn't just guessing? What if they had access to a detailed report about your shopping habits, preferences, and even your private conversations? In the digital world, this scenario isn't hypothetical; it's the reality of surveillance capitalism.

Surveillance capitalism is a term that describes how companies profit by collecting and analysing personal data. At its core, it's an economic system where your actions, online and sometimes offline, are turned into data points, analysed, and then sold or used to predict and influence future behaviour. While it might sound like a harmless business model, the implications are far-reaching and deeply embedded in our everyday lives.

Companies like Google, Facebook, and Amazon have built empires on the foundation of surveillance capitalism. Their business models revolve around collecting as much data as possible, analysing it, and using it to create hyper-targeted ads or personalized experiences. On the surface, it might seem like a win-win: users get free services, and companies get the data they need to improve their offerings. But as we'll explore in this chapter, the true cost of these "free" services is often hidden and can have significant consequences for individuals and society as a whole.

One of the most striking aspects of surveillance capitalism is how seamlessly it operates. Most of us don't even realize how much data we're sharing. Every search query, social media like, and GPS location contributes to a vast pool of information that companies use to profile us. These profiles aren't just static records of who we are; they're dynamic tools designed to predict what we'll do next. From the ads we see to the news articles recommended to us, surveillance capitalism shapes our digital experiences in ways we rarely notice.

But how exactly does this system work? It all starts with data collection. Companies use tools like cookies, apps, and sensors to gather information about everything from your browsing habits to your physical location. This data is then fed into algorithms that analyse patterns and generate insights. The end result? Highly accurate behavioural predictions that companies can use to target ads, sell products, or even influence decisions.

While surveillance capitalism has undoubtedly driven innovation and convenience, it's not without controversy. Critics argue that turning personal data into a commodity raises serious ethical questions. For example, is it fair to profit from someone's private information without their explicit consent? And what happens when these systems are used to manipulate behaviour or exploit vulnerabilities? These are questions we'll delve into as we explore the inner workings of this economic model.

This chapter will also highlight real-world examples of how surveillance capitalism impacts our lives. From Google's search engine to Facebook's targeted advertising platform, we'll examine how some of the world's largest companies use data to generate billions of dollars in revenue. We'll also look at the ethical dilemmas these practices raise and discuss what can be done to create a more balanced digital economy.

By the end of this chapter, you'll have a clear understanding of what surveillance capitalism is, how it works, and why it matters. You'll also gain insights into the ways your data is being used and what you can do to protect your privacy in an increasingly data-driven world.

What is Surveillance Capitalism?

Surveillance capitalism is an economic system where personal data is the primary resource. Companies collect this data, analyse it, and use it to predict and influence human behaviour. Unlike traditional capitalism, where tangible goods like cars or furniture are bought and sold, surveillance capitalism revolves around intangible assets: your data and attention.

The term "surveillance capitalism" was popularized by Shoshana Zuboff, a Harvard professor and author of The Age of Surveillance Capitalism. She describes it as a "new economic order" that claims private human experience as a free source of raw material. This raw material is then used to create predictive products, tools that forecast what people will do, buy, or think.

At the heart of surveillance capitalism is the idea that personal data has immense value. For companies, knowing what a person wants, needs, or fears provides a competitive advantage. By analysing data from millions of users, companies can uncover patterns and trends that would otherwise be invisible. These insights are then used to develop targeted marketing strategies, improve product designs, or even create entirely new services.

How Behavioural Profiling and Predictive Algorithms Work

Behavioural profiling is one of the key components of surveillance capitalism. It involves collecting data about an individual's actions, preferences, and habits to create a detailed profile of who they are. This profile is then used to predict future behaviour.

For example, let's say you frequently search for healthy recipes online, visit fitness websites, and follow wellness influencers on social media. Based on this behaviour, companies might profile you as someone who is health-conscious. This profile can then be used to show you ads for gym memberships, organic food, or workout equipment.

Predictive algorithms take this concept a step further. These algorithms analyse your data and use it to forecast what you're likely to do next. For instance, if you've been searching for hiking gear, an algorithm might predict that you're planning a trip and start showing you ads for travel destinations or outdoor clothing.

One of the reasons these algorithms are so effective is that they operate on a massive scale. By analysing data from millions of users, they can identify patterns that are statistically significant. This allows companies to make highly accurate predictions, even about individuals they've never interacted with before.

Data Auctions and Real-Time Bidding

Data auctions are another critical element of surveillance capitalism. In these auctions, companies bid on user data in real time to deliver targeted ads. Here's how it works:

When you visit a website, data about your activity (e.g., what you're reading, your location, and your browsing history) is sent to an ad exchange.

Advertisers on the exchange analyse this data and decide how much they're willing to pay to show you an ad.

The highest bidder wins, and their ad is displayed to you within milliseconds.

This process, known as real-time bidding, happens behind the scenes every time you load a webpage. It's a highly efficient system that allows advertisers to reach specific audiences with pinpoint accuracy.

For example, if you're reading an article about electric cars, an advertiser might bid to show you an ad for a Tesla. If you're browsing a travel website, you might see ads for hotels or airline tickets. The goal is to match the ad to your immediate interests, increasing the likelihood that you'll click on it.

Case Studies: Real-World Examples of Surveillance Capitalism

Google: The King of Data

Google is often cited as the most prominent example of surveillance capitalism. The company collects data from a wide range of sources, including its search engine, Gmail, YouTube, and Android devices. This data is used to create detailed user profiles that power Google's advertising platform, which generates billions of dollars in revenue each year.

For instance, when you use Google Search, the company records what you're looking for, how you phrase your queries, and which links you click on. This information helps Google deliver more relevant search results and, more importantly, more targeted ads.

Facebook: The Social Media Giant

Facebook operates on a similar model, using data from its platform to create hyper-targeted advertising campaigns. Every like, comment, and share contributes to your digital profile, which advertisers can use to target you with incredible precision. For example, if you've liked pages about running, you might see ads for running shoes or marathon events.

Ethical Concerns and the Commodification of Data

While surveillance capitalism has driven innovation, it's also raised serious ethical questions. One of the most significant concerns is the commodification of personal data. Turning human experiences into a product to be bought and sold blurs the line between public and private life. Critics argue that this practice exploits individuals, often without their informed consent.

Another issue is the lack of transparency. Most people don't fully understand how their data is being used or who has access to it. This lack of awareness makes it difficult for individuals to make informed decisions about their privacy.

Finally, there's the risk of manipulation. By using data to predict and influence behaviour, companies can exploit vulnerabilities or reinforce biases. For example, targeted ads for payday loans might disproportionately appear to individuals facing financial difficulties, perpetuating cycles of debt.

Conclusion

Surveillance capitalism is a powerful economic model that has reshaped the digital landscape. While it has enabled incredible advancements in technology and convenience, it also comes with significant risks. By understanding how this system works and recognizing its ethical implications, we can begin to take steps toward a more balanced and equitable digital economy. As users, our awareness and choices play a crucial role in shaping the future of data privacy and security.

Government Surveillance and Privacy

Imagine a world where every email you send, every phone call you make, and every website you visit is tracked, analysed, and stored by a government agency. For many people, this might sound like the plot of a dystopian novel, but it is closer to reality than most of us realize. Government surveillance is not a new phenomenon, but the digital age has given it unprecedented reach and power. While governments argue that surveillance is necessary for national security and public safety, it comes at the cost of individual privacy and freedom.

The relationship between governments and surveillance is complex and often controversial. On one hand, surveillance can help prevent terrorism, solve crimes, and protect citizens from harm. On the other hand, it raises significant ethical concerns about how much power governments should have over the lives of their citizens. History has shown us that unchecked surveillance can lead to abuses of power, suppression of dissent, and violations of human rights.

To understand government surveillance in the digital age, we need to look at its evolution. Early forms of surveillance, like wiretapping and phone bugging, were labour-intensive and targeted specific individuals. Today, surveillance has become mass-scale, automated, and far more invasive. Governments now collect vast amounts of data on millions of people, often without their knowledge or consent. This data includes everything from metadata (information about your communications, like who you talk to and when) to the actual content of your messages.

One of the most significant turning points in the history of government surveillance came in 2013, when Edward Snowden, a former contractor for the National Security Agency (NSA), revealed the extent of mass surveillance programs run by the United States and its allies. Snowden's disclosures showed that governments were not just spying on suspected criminals or terrorists but on ordinary citizens, world leaders, and even their own allies. These revelations sparked a global debate about the balance between security and privacy.

In this chapter, we'll explore the tools and methods governments use for surveillance, from collecting metadata to breaking encryption. We'll examine case studies like the Snowden revelations and the FBI's dispute with Apple over encrypted iPhones. We'll also look at privacy laws and regulations, comparing approaches in different parts of the world and discussing their effectiveness. Finally, we'll address the critical question: how can we balance the need for security with the fundamental right to privacy?

Government surveillance is a topic that affects everyone, whether you realize it or not. Every time you use your smartphone, browse the web, or send an email, there is a chance that your actions are being monitored. Understanding how this surveillance works and its implications is the first step toward protecting your privacy and advocating for a more transparent and accountable system. Let's dive into the world of government surveillance and explore what it means for you and your digital life.

The Evolution of Government Surveillance: From Wiretapping to Mass Data Collection

Government surveillance has come a long way since the days of wiretapping and phone bugging. In the early 20th century, surveillance was largely a manual process that involved physically intercepting communications. For example, during World War II, governments tapped phone lines and intercepted letters to gather intelligence. While these methods were effective, they were also time-consuming and required significant resources.

The rise of electronic communication in the late 20th century changed everything. With the advent of email, mobile phones, and the internet, governments gained access to a wealth of new data. Intercepting a phone call or reading an email became much easier than tapping a landline or opening a letter. As technology advanced, so did the tools and techniques used for surveillance.

One of the most significant developments in modern surveillance is the use of metadata. Metadata is information about your communications rather than the content itself. For example, metadata from a phone call includes the phone numbers involved, the duration of the call, and the time it took place. While metadata may seem less intrusive than content, it can reveal a great deal about your habits, relationships, and activities. Governments often justify collecting metadata by arguing that it is less sensitive than content, but critics point out that it can be just as revealing.

Another key development is the use of automated surveillance systems. Unlike traditional methods that required human operators, modern systems rely on algorithms and artificial intelligence to analyse vast amounts of data. For example, programs like PRISM and XKeyscore, revealed by Edward Snowden, allow governments to monitor emails, social media activity, and browsing histories on an unprecedented scale.

The sophistication of surveillance tools continues to grow. Governments now use advanced technologies like machine learning to identify patterns and anomalies in vast datasets. These systems can flag potential threats based on subtle behavioural cues that would be impossible for humans to detect. While this approach has improved the efficiency of surveillance, it also raises concerns about accuracy and fairness. False positives can result in innocent individuals being wrongly targeted, with potentially devastating consequences.

Tools and Methods of Government Surveillance

Governments use a variety of tools and methods to monitor their citizens. These include:

Metadata Collection: As mentioned earlier, metadata provides information about communications without revealing their content. This data is often collected in bulk, allowing governments to analyse patterns and identify potential threats. Metadata can include the time and location of a call, the recipients of emails, and even the devices used.

Backdoors: Governments sometimes pressure technology companies to create backdoors in their products, allowing authorities to bypass encryption and access user data. While backdoors are intended for law enforcement, they can also be exploited by hackers. The debate over backdoors highlights the tension between security and privacy, as their presence weakens the overall security of digital systems.

Encryption-Breaking Methods: Some governments invest heavily in technologies to break encryption. This involves using powerful computers to crack encryption algorithms or finding vulnerabilities in encryption software. For example, quantum computing, though still in its infancy, has the potential to render current encryption methods obsolete.

Surveillance Cameras and Facial Recognition: In many cities, surveillance cameras equipped with facial recognition software are used to monitor public spaces. These systems can track individuals in real-time and identify them based on their facial features. Countries like China have implemented extensive facial recognition systems that link individuals to their digital and physical activities.

Internet and Social Media Monitoring: Governments often monitor online activity, including social media posts, search queries, and website visits. This data can be used to identify dissent, track movements, or predict behaviour. Social media platforms, which collect vast amounts of personal data, are particularly valuable sources of information for surveillance.

Communication Interception: Wiretapping, email monitoring, and SMS interception remain common methods of surveillance. With the rise of encrypted messaging apps like WhatsApp and Signal, governments have sought ways to access these communications, often citing national security concerns.

Case Studies: Real-World Examples of Government Surveillance

The Snowden Revelations

In 2013, Edward Snowden leaked classified documents that revealed the extent of surveillance programs run by the NSA and its allies. These programs included PRISM, which allowed the NSA to access data from major tech companies like Google, Facebook, and Apple, and XKeyscore, a tool that enabled the agency to search and analyse vast amounts of internet data. Snowden's disclosures showed that these programs were not limited to targeting terrorists or criminals; they also spied on ordinary citizens, journalists, and even foreign leaders.

The impact of Snowden's revelations was profound. They prompted widespread public outrage, led to legal challenges against surveillance programs, and sparked debates about the balance between security and privacy. Many countries introduced new privacy laws in response to the disclosures, but the global surveillance infrastructure remains largely intact.

The FBI vs. Apple

In 2016, the FBI demanded that Apple unlock an iPhone used by one of the perpetrators of a terrorist attack in San Bernardino, California. Apple refused, arguing that creating a backdoor would compromise the security of all iPhone users. The case sparked a heated debate about the balance between security and privacy. While the FBI eventually accessed the phone using a third-party tool, the dispute highlighted the challenges of balancing law enforcement needs with individual privacy.

The Apple case also underscored the importance of encryption in protecting user data. Privacy advocates argue that weakening encryption for law enforcement creates vulnerabilities that can be exploited by malicious actors, putting everyone's data at risk.

Privacy Laws and Regulations

Different countries have taken different approaches to privacy laws and regulations. Some of the most notable include:

GDPR (Europe): The General Data Protection Regulation is one of the most comprehensive privacy laws in the world. It gives individuals greater control over their data and imposes strict requirements on companies to protect user information. Under GDPR, companies must obtain explicit consent to collect data, and individuals have the right to access, correct, and delete their data.

CCPA (California): The California Consumer Privacy Act provides similar protections to GDPR but applies specifically to residents of California. It allows users to opt out of data collection and requires companies to disclose how they use personal data. CCPA has been praised for setting a new standard for privacy in the United States.

Global Differences: While the EU and California have robust privacy laws, other regions, like Asia and the Middle East, often prioritize government surveillance over individual privacy. This creates significant disparities in how privacy is protected worldwide. For example, countries like China and Russia have implemented laws that grant governments extensive access to personal data, often with minimal oversight.

The Balance Between Security and Privacy

One of the most challenging aspects of government surveillance is finding the right balance between security and privacy. Governments argue that surveillance is necessary to prevent terrorism, combat crime, and protect citizens. However, critics point out that excessive surveillance can erode civil liberties and create a culture of fear.

For example, mass surveillance programs often operate with little transparency or oversight, making it difficult to hold governments accountable for abuses. Additionally, the sheer volume of data collected can lead to false positives and wrongful targeting, harming innocent people. There is also the risk of mission creep, where surveillance systems initially implemented for specific purposes are expanded to monitor other activities.

On the other hand, privacy advocates argue that strong encryption and robust privacy laws are essential to protect individuals from both government overreach and cybercriminals. They emphasize that privacy is a fundamental human right that should not be sacrificed in the name of security.

Finding the right balance requires robust legal frameworks, independent oversight, and public awareness. Transparency about how surveillance programs operate and safeguards to prevent abuse are critical for maintaining trust in government institutions.

Conclusion

Government surveillance is a double-edged sword. While it can enhance security and protect citizens, it also raises significant ethical and practical concerns. Understanding how surveillance works and the tools governments use is crucial for making informed decisions about privacy and security. As we navigate the complexities of the digital age, it's essential to advocate for systems that balance the need for security with the fundamental right to privacy. After all, a society without privacy is a society without freedom.

The Myth and Reality of Cookies

You are at your favourite coffee shop. The barista remembers your name, your regular order, and even that you prefer almond milk in your latte. You feel welcomed and valued. Now imagine that the same coffee shop tracks every word you speak, records which table you sit at, and watches what books you read, all without explicitly telling you. That's essentially what cookies do in the digital world. They provide convenience but can also intrude on your privacy.

Cookies are one of the most misunderstood aspects of digital tracking. Most people encounter them daily, whether they realize it or not. Every time you see a pop-up asking you to "accept cookies" while browsing the internet, you're making a decision that affects how much of your activity can be tracked. But what are cookies, and why do websites use them? Are they inherently harmful, or is their reputation exaggerated?

To many, cookies seem like a sneaky way for websites to spy on you. However, not all cookies are created equal. Some are essential for websites to function properly, while others are designed specifically to monitor your behaviour and target you with ads. The challenge lies in distinguishing between these types and understanding how they work behind the scenes.

Cookies have become a central component of the internet's ecosystem. They enable websites to remember your login details, save items in your shopping cart, and deliver personalized experiences. Without cookies, your online interactions would feel disjointed and frustrating. Yet, they also enable something far more intrusive: cross-site tracking, where companies follow your activities across multiple websites to build a detailed profile of you.

In this chapter, we'll demystify cookies and explore their dual nature. We'll discuss what cookies are, the different types of cookies, and how they work. We'll also address some common myths about cookies and explain how they contribute to digital tracking. By the end of this chapter, you'll not only understand cookies but also feel empowered to manage them effectively to protect your privacy.

Whether you're tech-savvy or new to these concepts, this chapter is for you. Cookies are an unavoidable part of online life, but by understanding their purpose and impact, you can make informed decisions about how much of your data you're willing to share. Let's dive in and separate the myths from the reality of cookies.

What Are Cookies, and Why Do Websites Use Them?

Cookies are small text files stored on your device by websites you visit. Think of them as digital breadcrumbs that help websites remember certain information about you. For example, when you log into an online account and choose the "Remember Me" option, a cookie is created to save your login credentials. The next time you visit the site, the cookie tells the website who you are, so you don't have to log in again.

At their core, cookies are tools for improving user experience. They make websites more convenient and efficient by remembering your preferences, such as your language settings or the items in your shopping cart. Without cookies, every time you visited a site, you'd have to start from scratch, re-entering your information and preferences over and over again.

For example, imagine shopping online for a gift. You add several items to your cart but get distracted and close the browser. Without cookies, your shopping cart would be empty when you return. With cookies, the website remembers your selections, making it easier for you to pick up where you left off. This level of convenience is one of the main reasons cookies are so widely used.

Websites use cookies for three main reasons:

Functionality: To ensure that the website works as intended. For instance, cookies can keep track of items in your cart while you're shopping online or remember your login details for faster access.

Performance: To understand how users interact with the website, helping site owners optimize the experience. These cookies collect data on things like which pages are most visited, how long users stay on them, and what features they use.

Targeted Advertising: To track your behaviour and show you ads tailored to your interests. These cookies often follow you across multiple websites, building a profile of your preferences and habits. For example, searching for flights to Paris might lead to travel-related ads appearing on completely unrelated websites.

Types of Cookies

Not all cookies serve the same purpose. They can generally be divided into two categories: essential cookies and non-essential cookies.

Essential Cookies (Session Tracking)

Essential cookies are necessary for websites to function properly. They include:

Session Cookies: These are temporary cookies that expire once you close your browser. They keep track of your activity during a single session, such as filling out a form or navigating between pages.

Authentication Cookies: These cookies help websites recognize you once you've logged in, so you don't have to re-enter your username and password on every page.

For example, when you log into an online banking portal, session cookies ensure that your activities are secure and confined to that session. Without these cookies, logging in securely or completing transactions would be impossible.

Essential cookies don't typically raise privacy concerns because they aren't used to track your behaviour beyond the website you're visiting.

Non-Essential Cookies (Advertising and Analytics)

Non-essential cookies are used for purposes beyond basic functionality. They include:

Tracking Cookies: These monitor your behaviour across multiple websites to build a profile of your interests. For example, if you search for running shoes, tracking cookies might show you ads for sneakers on other websites.

Analytics Cookies: These collect data about how users interact with a website, such as which pages they visit and how long they stay. While these cookies are used to improve websites, they also gather detailed information about user behaviour.

Non-essential cookies are where privacy concerns arise. They're often set by third parties, such as advertising networks, rather than the website you're visiting. A prime example is Facebook's tracking pixel, which allows businesses to retarget users based on their activity on other websites.

Myths About Cookies: Are They Inherently Harmful?

Cookies often get a bad reputation, but it's important to separate fact from fiction. Here are some common myths about cookies:

Myth: Cookies are viruses that can harm your device.

Reality: Cookies are plain text files and cannot execute code or spread malware. However, they can be used to track your online activity, which raises privacy concerns.

Myth: Deleting cookies will stop all tracking.

Reality: While deleting cookies can reduce tracking, it won't stop it entirely. Techniques like fingerprinting and server-side tracking don't rely on cookies. For instance, even if you block cookies, your browser's unique configuration (fonts, plugins, screen resolution) can still be used to identify and track you.

Myth: All cookies are bad.

Reality: Many cookies are harmless and even necessary for websites to function properly. The problem arises when cookies are used to invade your privacy. For example, cookies that store your language preference or shopping cart items improve usability without compromising your security.

How Cookies Track Users Across Websites

Cookies become particularly intrusive when they enable cross-site tracking. This happens when third-party cookies are used to follow your activity across multiple websites. Here's how it works:

You visit a website that displays ads from an advertising network.

The advertising network sets a cookie on your browser.

As you visit other websites that use the same advertising network, the cookie tracks your activity and updates your profile.

Based on this profile, the network shows you targeted ads that align with your interests.

For example, let's say you browse a website about vacation destinations. Later, you notice ads for hotels and flights popping up on unrelated sites. This is cross-site tracking in action.

Real-world example: Imagine searching for a coffee machine on Amazon. Later, you visit a news website and see ads for coffee brands or accessories. This happens because the advertising networks on both websites are sharing information about your interests.

Managing Cookies: Browser Settings, Cookie Blockers, and Consent Management

Fortunately, you have tools to manage cookies and protect your privacy. Here are some steps you can take:

Adjust Browser Settings:

Most browsers allow you to block third-party cookies, delete existing cookies, or prevent websites from setting any cookies.

Example: In Google Chrome, go to Settings > Privacy and Security > Cookies and Other Site Data.

In Safari, users can enable "Prevent Cross-Site Tracking" to block third-party cookies.

Use Cookie Blockers:

Extensions like uBlock Origin or Privacy Badger can block tracking cookies and other intrusive elements. These tools are especially useful for preventing ads that rely on cross-site tracking.

Review Consent Forms:

When a website asks you to accept cookies, take the time to customize your preferences. Many websites allow you to reject non-essential cookies while still using their basic features.

<u>Clear Cookies Regularly:</u>

Periodically delete cookies to remove old tracking data. This can be done through your browser's settings or using privacy-focused tools like CCleaner.

BUT: Since companies want your data at all costs, if you restrict the use of cookies, some of the website you may want to visit may not work as expected any more. I am not saying that these companies do this on purpose but it smells fishy.

Conclusion

Cookies are a double-edged sword. On one hand, they make the internet more convenient by remembering your preferences and improving user experiences. On the other hand, they enable intrusive tracking that raises significant privacy concerns. By understanding what cookies are and how they work, you can make informed decisions about how to manage them. Remember, you don't have to accept every cookie, you have the power to control your digital footprint. In the end, striking a balance between convenience and privacy is key to navigating the modern internet.

The Anatomy of a Data Breach

In the interconnected digital world, data breaches have become a stark reminder of how vulnerable our personal and corporate information truly is. Every headline about millions of accounts compromised or sensitive records exposed underlines the pressing need for stronger digital defences. But how do these breaches happen? What does it mean when a company announces that sensitive customer data has been leaked? These questions aren't just for IT professionals or corporate executives; they affect every one of us who interacts with the internet.

A data breach is not a single event but a series of actions, intentional or accidental, that result in sensitive data falling into unauthorized hands. Whether it's a phishing email, an overlooked software update, or even an employee's mistake, the pathways to a breach are numerous. What follows can be devastating: financial losses, identity theft, reputational harm, and even national security risks.

Take, for instance, the Equifax breach in 2017, which exposed the personal information of over 147 million people. This breach wasn't the result of a sophisticated hacking effort but a failure to patch a known vulnerability. On the other hand, the Yahoo breach, the largest in history, was the product of a sustained attack over years, compromising more than three billion accounts.

This chapter takes a deep dive into the anatomy of a data breach. By breaking down the methods hackers use, the role of human error, and the ripple effects on individuals and corporations, we aim to provide a comprehensive understanding of these events. Additionally, we'll analyse notable breaches, highlighting lessons learned and actionable steps to prevent future incidents.

More importantly, we'll empower you with tools and strategies to protect your personal data and mitigate damage if your information is ever compromised. Data breaches may be an inevitable part of the digital age, but understanding their mechanics is the first step toward minimizing their impact. Let's explore how breaches occur, their consequences, and what you can do to safeguard your digital presence.

How Data Breaches Occur

Data breaches happen when unauthorized individuals gain access to sensitive data, whether through malicious intent, negligence, or unforeseen vulnerabilities. Let's break down the main ways these breaches occur:

Hacking: Exploiting System Vulnerabilities

Hacking is perhaps the most recognizable cause of data breaches. Hackers often exploit flaws in software, weak security configurations, or unsecured networks to infiltrate systems. Common hacking methods include:

SQL Injection:
This technique targets databases by injecting malicious code into a website's input fields, bypassing authentication and gaining access to sensitive data. For example, poorly secured login pages are often vulnerable to such attacks.

Malware:
Hackers deploy malicious software like spyware, ransomware, or keyloggers to infiltrate systems. In ransomware attacks, hackers encrypt files and demand payment in exchange for the decryption key. The 2021 Colonial Pipeline attack, which disrupted fuel supplies in the United States, was one such incident.

Brute Force Attacks:
These involve automated tools that guess passwords by trying every possible combination. Weak passwords, like "123456" or "password," make this method alarmingly effective.

In 2019, a hacking group exploited weak passwords to access Microsoft email accounts, targeting businesses and individuals alike. The breach exposed emails and sensitive attachments, highlighting the importance of strong password policies.

Phishing: Deception as a Weapon

Phishing is a form of social engineering that tricks individuals into divulging sensitive information, such as usernames, passwords, or credit card details. Phishing emails often impersonate trusted entities, like banks or popular websites, and create a sense of urgency to prompt immediate action.

For example, a phishing email might claim there's been unauthorized activity on your account and urge you to click a link to verify your credentials. Once you enter your information, it's harvested by the attacker.

In 2020, a phishing scam targeting employees of a major hospital system compromised thousands of accounts. The attackers used fake emails claiming to be from IT support, tricking staff into revealing login details.

Human Error: The Weakest Link

Not all breaches are caused by malicious actors. Human error plays a significant role in data breaches. Common mistakes include:

Misconfigured Cloud Storage: In 2020, over 250 million Microsoft customer support records were exposed due to a misconfigured cloud database, leaving sensitive data publicly accessible.

Weak Passwords: Reusing or choosing simple passwords remains a widespread issue, enabling hackers to gain access to multiple accounts.

Insider Mistakes: Employees sometimes inadvertently email sensitive information to the wrong recipient or leave devices unsecured.

Consequences for Individuals and Corporations

The fallout from a data breach can be devastating for individuals:

Identity Theft: Hackers can use stolen personal information to open fraudulent accounts, apply for loans, or file fake tax returns.

Financial Loss: Unauthorized charges, drained accounts, and fraudulent transactions can wreak havoc on personal finances.

Emotional Impact: Victims often experience anxiety and stress, particularly when deeply personal information, like medical records, is exposed.

Real-world impact: The 2015 Anthem breach exposed medical records of nearly 80 million individuals. Victims faced not only financial fraud but also concerns about their private health information being misused.

For Corporations:

Financial Costs: Beyond fines and settlements, companies face expenses for forensic investigations, legal battles, and customer notifications. Equifax's breach settlement exceeded $700 million.

Reputational Damage: Customers lose trust in companies that fail to protect their data. Yahoo's mishandling of its breach contributed to its decline as a tech giant.

Operational Disruption: Ransomware attacks can paralyze operations, costing millions in downtime and lost productivity.

Regulatory Scrutiny: Companies may face increased oversight and tighter regulations after a breach.

Case Studies: Major Data Breaches

Equifax Breach (2017)

Equifax, one of the largest credit reporting agencies, suffered a breach that exposed the personal information of 147 million people. Hackers exploited a known vulnerability in the company's web application software. The exposed data included Social Security numbers, birth dates, and credit card details. Equifax's failure to implement timely software updates underscored the importance of proactive cybersecurity measures.

Yahoo Breach (2013-2014)

Yahoo's breaches remain the largest in history, compromising over 3 billion accounts. The stolen information included email addresses, passwords, and security questions. Yahoo's delayed disclosure further eroded customer trust, contributing to its sale to Verizon at a reduced price.

Marriott Breach (2018)

Hackers accessed Marriott's Starwood database, compromising the personal information of 500 million guests. The breach included passport numbers, credit card details, and travel itineraries. Marriott's failure to detect the breach for four years highlighted the importance of regular security audits.

How to Protect Yourself

Protecting yourself from data breaches begins with understanding the risks and taking proactive steps to safeguard your digital presence. Many breaches result from weak personal security practices or falling victim to phishing scams. By adopting basic but effective habits, you can significantly reduce your vulnerability.

The first step is recognizing that no system is foolproof, and breaches can happen even to the most cautious individuals. However, you can make yourself a harder target. Think of digital security like locking your front door, while it might not deter a highly skilled burglar, it will stop opportunistic attackers looking for easy access.

It's also important to stay informed. Many breaches occur because users are unaware of the latest threats or fail to update their software in time. Regularly reading about cybersecurity trends and news can help you stay ahead of potential risks. This knowledge is particularly useful when identifying phishing attempts or unusual activity in your accounts.

Finally, investing in the right tools can make a significant difference. Password managers, two-factor authentication, and antivirus software are just a few examples of tools that can enhance your security. Combined with good habits, these tools create multiple layers of protection that make it much harder for hackers to breach your data.

Password Management

- Use strong, unique passwords for every account. A strong password includes uppercase and lowercase letters, numbers, and symbols.
- Use a password manager to securely store and generate passwords.
- Avoid reusing passwords across multiple accounts.

Two-Factor Authentication (2FA)

- Enable 2FA whenever possible. This adds a second layer of security by requiring a code sent to your phone or email.

- Example: Even if a hacker obtains your password, they cannot access your account without the second verification.

Steps to Take After a Breach

- Change Your Passwords: Immediately update passwords for affected accounts.
- Monitor Your Accounts: Regularly check bank statements and email activity for unauthorized actions.
- Place Fraud Alerts: Notify credit bureaus to flag your account for potential fraud.
- Freeze Your Credit: Prevent new accounts from being opened in your name by freezing your credit with major bureaus.
- Use Identity Theft Protection Services: Services like LifeLock monitor your information and alert you to potential fraud.

Conclusion

Data breaches are a stark reality of our interconnected world, but understanding how they happen and their consequences can empower you to protect yourself. By adopting best practices, staying vigilant, and taking proactive measures, you can minimize your risk and respond effectively if your data is ever compromised. Knowledge is power, and in the digital age, it's your best defines.

Digital Tracking: How You Are Followed Online

Every day, you leave a digital trail behind without even realizing it. From the moment you check your phone in the morning to the time you stream a movie before bed, countless entities are watching, recording, and analysing your activities. Companies track your behaviour to show you ads tailored to your interests, optimize their services, and, most importantly, make a profit. But how exactly does this tracking work? And is it really as pervasive as it sounds?

Digital tracking is everywhere. It's in the cookies stored in your browser, the unique fingerprint of your device, and even the location data from your phone. Websites, apps, and advertisers use sophisticated tools to follow your online movements, learn about your preferences, and predict your next actions. While some of this tracking is innocuous and even helpful, like remembering your shopping cart or suggesting relevant articles, a large portion is invasive, conducted without your explicit knowledge or consent.

Take, for example, the concept of targeted advertising. Have you ever searched for a product online, only to see ads for it follow you across multiple websites? This isn't a coincidence; it's a direct result of digital tracking.

Companies use tools like tracking pixels and cookies to monitor your online activity, building a profile of your interests and habits. This profile is then used to serve ads that are more likely to grab your attention.

But digital tracking goes beyond advertising. It influences the news articles you read, the videos you watch, and even the prices you see for products online. This raises important questions about privacy, autonomy, and the ethics of using personal data for profit. Should companies have the right to collect and use your data without your full understanding? And what can you do to take back control of your digital life?

In this chapter, we'll break down the mechanics of digital tracking, explaining how it works and the tools companies use to follow you. We'll also explore how tracking shapes your online experience, from personalized content to behavioural manipulation. Finally, we'll provide actionable steps to detect and block tracking, empowering you to navigate the digital world with greater confidence and privacy.

By the end of this chapter, you'll not only understand how pervasive digital tracking is but also feel equipped to minimize its impact on your life. Knowledge is your most powerful tool in the fight for digital privacy. Let's uncover the hidden mechanics of how you're being followed online.

How Tracking Works

Digital tracking is the backbone of modern online ecosystems, enabling websites and companies to monitor user behaviour in granular detail. Every click, search, and scroll generates data points that can be pieced together to create a detailed picture of who you are, what you do, and even what you might do next. These tracking systems are intricately designed to be efficient and, often, invisible. Most people aren't even aware of how much information they are giving away simply by browsing the internet or using an app.

The complexity of digital tracking lies in the variety of techniques used to collect data. From basic methods like cookies to advanced systems like device fingerprinting, tracking operates at multiple levels to ensure no user slips through the cracks. Websites and advertisers can integrate these tools seamlessly into their platforms, creating a constant feedback loop of data collection and personalization. By understanding these mechanisms, as well as the principles discussed in earlier chapters, it becomes clear why digital privacy is so challenging to protect in the age of ubiquitous tracking.

IP Addresses

Every device connected to the internet is assigned an Internet Protocol (IP) address. This unique identifier acts like a digital home address, allowing websites and services to know where requests are coming from. While your IP address doesn't reveal your exact location, it can provide a general idea, such as your city or region. For example, when you visit a weather website, it uses your IP address to display local forecasts.

However, IP addresses can also be used for tracking. Advertisers and analytics companies often log IP addresses to monitor user activity across different websites. In some cases, combining IP data with other information can reveal detailed insights about a user's behaviour and identity.

In Chapter 1, we discussed the foundational role of digital privacy and why even basic identifiers like IP addresses can compromise your anonymity. Without tools to mask or rotate your IP, you're essentially handing companies a breadcrumb trail they can easily follow.

Device Fingerprints
Device fingerprinting is a more advanced tracking method that collects information about your device's unique characteristics. This includes details like your browser type, operating system, screen resolution, installed fonts, and even the hardware specifications of your device. By combining these attributes,

companies can create a "fingerprint" that uniquely identifies your device, even if you clear your cookies or use incognito mode.

For example, a retail website might use device fingerprinting to recognize returning visitors and show them personalized offers. While this can improve user experience, it also raises privacy concerns because it's difficult to detect or block. Device fingerprinting highlights why Chapter 2's exploration of surveillance capitalism warned us about how companies exploit technological sophistication to make data collection seamless and unavoidable.

Browser Cookies

As discussed in Chapter 4, cookies are small text files stored on your device by websites you visit. While some cookies are essential for website functionality, others are used for tracking your activity across multiple sites. Third-party cookies, in particular, are often set by advertisers to monitor your behaviour and serve targeted ads.

For instance, if you visit a travel website and search for flights, cookies from an advertising network might record this activity. Later, when you visit a news website that partners with the same network, you might see ads for hotels or vacation packages based on your earlier search. This is why controlling cookies, as we outlined earlier, is critical for reducing your exposure to unnecessary tracking.

Tools Companies Use

Companies employ a variety of sophisticated tools to track user behaviour and gather data, often operating in ways that are invisible to the average user. These tools are designed not only to monitor your activity but also to collect data across different platforms, devices, and interactions, creating a comprehensive profile of who you are.

The tools used for tracking range from simple technologies, like cookies, to highly advanced systems like device fingerprinting and artificial intelligence-powered algorithms. Their effectiveness lies in their ability to integrate data from multiple sources, providing companies with detailed insights into your habits, preferences, and even your potential future behaviour. For example, by combining data from a fitness app, an online retailer, and your social media activity, companies can infer your lifestyle choices and tailor their marketing efforts accordingly.

Many of these tracking tools are also embedded in third-party services that websites and apps rely on for analytics, advertising, or functionality. This means even if you avoid directly interacting with certain companies, they may still have access to your data through partnerships or shared networks. Tools like beacons, geofencing, and tracking pixels are particularly effective because they work behind the scenes, often without requiring explicit user consent. Understanding these tools is crucial to making informed decisions about your digital privacy.

Below, we'll explore some of the most common tools companies use to track users, how they function, and the implications they have for your privacy:

Beacons

Beacons are tiny, invisible images embedded in websites or emails. When you load a webpage or open an email containing a beacon, it sends a request to the server, notifying it that the content has been viewed. Beacons can track whether you've opened an email, how long you've spent on a webpage, and what actions you've taken.

For example, a marketing email from an online retailer might contain a beacon to track whether you've opened the email and clicked on any links. This information helps the company measure the effectiveness of its campaigns.

Geofencing

Geofencing uses GPS, Wi-Fi, or cellular data to define a virtual boundary around a specific geographic area. When a user enters or exits this area, it triggers an action, such as sending a notification or logging their location. Geofencing is commonly used in mobile apps for location-based marketing.

For instance, a retail app might send you a coupon when you walk past one of its stores. While this can be convenient, it also raises privacy concerns, as it requires constant location tracking. This constant tracking ties back to Chapter 3's discussion of government surveillance, as geofencing technology is sometimes used by law enforcement to monitor specific areas.

Tracking Pixels

Tracking pixels are similar to beacons but are often used specifically for advertising. These tiny, invisible elements are embedded in web pages or emails to collect data about user interactions. For example, a tracking pixel on an e-commerce website might record which products you've viewed, allowing advertisers to show you ads for those products later.

How Tracking Influences Behaviour

Digital tracking doesn't just monitor your activity; it actively shapes the way you experience the online world. Whether it's the articles you read, the ads you see, or the suggestions you receive, companies use tracking data to create an environment tailored to your preferences. However, this customization is often designed to benefit the companies themselves, not necessarily the users.

One significant way tracking influences behaviour is through targeted advertising. Companies analyse your browsing history, search queries, and even your location to determine what products or services you're most likely to buy. This ensures that the ads you see are not random but specifically chosen to capture your attention. While this might seem convenient, it also means you're constantly being nudged towards making purchasing decisions, often without realizing the extent to which your choices are being shaped.

Another area heavily impacted by tracking is content recommendation. Platforms like YouTube, Netflix, and social media sites rely on algorithms to suggest videos, articles, or posts based on your past interactions. While this can enhance your experience by making it easier to find relevant content, it can also create echo chambers that reinforce existing opinions or habits. For example, someone who frequently watches videos about a particular political viewpoint might find their feed dominated by similar content, limiting exposure to diverse perspectives.

Tracking doesn't just influence what you see; it can also affect how much you pay. Dynamic pricing, a practice where companies adjust prices based on user behaviour, is a direct result of tracking. Airlines, for instance, often use cookies to monitor how frequently you search for a particular flight. If the system detects repeated interest, it might raise the price, encouraging you to book quickly. These subtle manipulations can have a profound impact on how users perceive value and make decisions.

By understanding how tracking shapes your behaviour, you can begin to recognize when you're being influenced and take steps to regain control over your online experience. The next section will explore practical strategies to detect and block tracking, ensuring that your digital environment works for you, not against you.

Tools for Digital Anonymity

In a world where your every move online is monitored, tracked, and monetized, the quest for digital anonymity has never been more critical. Imagine walking down a crowded street with a spotlight following your every step, that's what browsing the internet feels like without protective tools. Every click, search, and login creates a data point that companies, advertisers, and even governments can use to paint a detailed picture of your life. For those who value their privacy, the solution lies in equipping themselves with the right tools to take back control.

The tools for digital anonymity act like shields, protecting you from prying eyes and invasive trackers. Whether it's a Virtual Private Network (VPN) that masks your IP address or a privacy-focused browser that blocks cookies, these tools are designed to help you reclaim your digital freedom. But choosing the right tool for the job can be overwhelming. With so many options available, how do you know what works best for your specific needs?

Moreover, using these tools effectively requires more than just downloading an app. For example, a VPN won't protect you from all tracking if you're still signed into your social media accounts or using the same email address everywhere. Similarly, encrypted messaging apps can safeguard your conversations, but only if both you and the recipient are using them. Digital anonymity isn't just about tools, it's about adopting the right habits and understanding the trade-offs between convenience and privacy.

In this chapter, we'll explore some of the most powerful tools for maintaining anonymity online. From VPNs and Tor to privacy-focused browsers and encrypted email services, each tool offers unique benefits and use cases. We'll also delve into how to use these tools effectively, ensuring that you get the most protection possible. Additionally, we'll discuss the trade-offs you might encounter, after all, achieving complete anonymity often comes at the cost of convenience or speed.

By the end of this chapter, you'll have a toolkit of resources to protect your digital identity and feel empowered to make informed decisions about your privacy. While no tool can guarantee 100% anonymity, combining them with mindful online behaviour can significantly reduce your exposure to tracking and surveillance. Let's dive into the world of digital privacy tools and discover how to shield yourself in an increasingly transparent online world.

Overview of Tools

Digital anonymity begins with understanding the tools at your disposal. Here, we'll break down the most widely used privacy tools, explaining what they do, how they work, and when to use them.

- Virtual Private Networks (VPNs)
  A VPN is one of the most popular tools for online privacy. It creates an encrypted tunnel between your device and the internet, masking your IP address and routing your traffic through a secure server. This makes it appear as though your connection is coming from a different location, protecting your identity and preventing websites from tracking your real IP address.

  For example, if you connect to a VPN server in Germany while sitting in the United States, websites will assume you're browsing from Germany. VPNs are especially useful for bypassing geographic restrictions, such as accessing streaming services or websites that are blocked in certain countries.

- Tor Browser
  The Tor browser takes anonymity a step further. Tor (The Onion Router) routes your internet traffic through a series of volunteer-operated servers, encrypting the data at every step. This makes it nearly impossible for anyone to trace your online activity back to you. Tor is often used by journalists, activists, and whistleblowers to access the internet securely in regions with heavy surveillance.

Unlike VPNs, Tor is specifically designed for anonymity, not speed. While it's slower than traditional browsers, it offers unparalleled protection for those who prioritize privacy over convenience.

- Privacy-Focused Browsers
  Browsers like Brave and Firefox are built with privacy in mind. Brave blocks ads, trackers, and third-party cookies by default, while Firefox offers extensive customization options for enhanced security. These browsers strike a balance between usability and privacy, making them ideal for everyday browsing.

  For example, Brave rewards users with cryptocurrency for viewing non-intrusive ads, creating a more ethical and user-friendly browsing experience. Firefox, on the other hand, allows users to install privacy-enhancing extensions like uBlock Origin or Privacy Badger for additional protection.

- Encrypted Email Services
  Traditional email providers like Gmail and Yahoo scan your emails to serve targeted ads. Encrypted email services like ProtonMail and Tutanota, however, prioritize user privacy. These services use end-to-end encryption to ensure that only the sender and recipient can read the contents of an email.

Even the service provider cannot access your messages.

Encrypted email is especially important for sensitive communications, such as sharing legal or financial information. With growing concerns about email privacy, these services offer a secure alternative to mainstream providers.

- Encrypted Messaging Apps
Messaging apps like Signal, Telegram, and WhatsApp use end-to-end encryption to protect your conversations from being intercepted. Signal is widely regarded as the gold standard for secure messaging, offering features like disappearing messages and encrypted voice and video calls.

While WhatsApp also uses end-to-end encryption, its parent company, Meta (formerly Facebook), raises concerns about data sharing. Signal, on the other hand, is a nonprofit organization dedicated solely to privacy, making it a trusted choice for those who value secure communication.

How to Use These Tools Effectively

Simply downloading privacy tools is not enough; you need to use them correctly to maximize their effectiveness. Here are some practical tips:

Combine Tools: Using multiple tools together provides layered protection. For instance, pairing a VPN with a privacy-focused browser like Brave ensures both your IP address and browsing activity are protected.

Choose Trusted Providers: Not all VPNs or encrypted email services are created equal. Research providers thoroughly, prioritizing those with transparent privacy policies and no-logs practices.

Stay Updated: Regularly update your tools to ensure they are equipped to handle the latest security threats.

Mind Your Habits: Even with privacy tools, avoid oversharing personal information online or using the same login credentials across multiple accounts.

Trade-offs: Convenience vs. Anonymity

While privacy tools offer significant benefits, they often come with trade-offs. Understanding these trade-offs helps you make informed decisions about when and how to use them.

Speed: Tools like Tor are slower than traditional browsing due to the multiple layers of encryption. If speed is critical, consider using a VPN instead.

Usability: Privacy-focused tools may lack the seamless user experience of mainstream alternatives. For example, encrypted email services may not integrate as easily with third-party apps.

Cost: Some tools, like premium VPNs or encrypted email services, require a subscription fee. While free options exist, they may come with limitations or ads.

Practical Example: A Fictional Account of Protecting Data

Let's consider a day in the life of Sarah, a freelance journalist. Concerned about online surveillance, Sarah uses a combination of tools to protect her data:

She starts her day by connecting to a VPN, masking her IP address while researching sensitive topics.

For her communication, Sarah uses Signal to discuss projects with her sources, ensuring their conversations remain private.

When she needs to send files, she relies on ProtonMail for secure email exchanges.

To browse the web, Sarah alternates between Tor for anonymity and Brave for general research, blocking trackers and ads along the way.

By integrating these tools into her routine, Sarah minimizes her digital footprint and safeguards her privacy without compromising productivity.

Setting Up a VPN: Step-by-Step Guide

- Choose a Provider: Research and select a reputable VPN provider with a no-logs policy.
- Download the App: Install the VPN app on your devices, such as your computer, phone, or tablet.
- Log In: Sign in to your account using the credentials provided by the VPN service.
- Connect to a Server: Select a server location and click "Connect." Your traffic will now be routed through the VPN.
- Test Your Connection: Use tools like "What Is My IP" to confirm that your IP address has changed.

Conclusion

Achieving digital anonymity requires more than just one tool; it's about creating a comprehensive strategy that integrates multiple layers of protection. While privacy tools like VPNs, Tor, and encrypted messaging apps can significantly enhance your security, they must be used correctly to be effective. Balancing convenience with anonymity is key, not every tool will fit every situation, but understanding your options allows you to make informed choices.

By adopting these tools and practices, you take a vital step toward reclaiming your privacy in an era of pervasive surveillance. The internet doesn't have to be a place where you're constantly watched. With the right tools and habits, you can navigate the digital world on your own terms.

IoT and Smart Devices: Privacy in the Connected Age

The Internet of Things (IoT) is changing the way we live, work, and interact with technology. From smart speakers that play our favourite songs to thermostats that learn our daily routines, IoT devices promise convenience and efficiency. But beneath their sleek designs and advanced features lies a critical concern: privacy. These devices, often connected to the internet 24/7, collect vast amounts of data about our lives, raising questions about who has access to this information and how it is used.

IoT devices are embedded in nearly every aspect of modern life. Smart refrigerators can notify you when you're running low on milk, wearable fitness trackers can monitor your health, and security cameras can stream live video to your phone. While these innovations make life more convenient, they also create new vulnerabilities. Hackers, corporations, and even governments can exploit these devices to gain unauthorized access to personal data or monitor user behaviour.

The privacy concerns surrounding IoT devices go beyond simple data collection. Many devices are designed with minimal security features, making them easy targets for cyberattacks. For example, poorly secured smart cameras have been hacked, allowing strangers to view private video feeds. Additionally, companies that manufacture these devices often collect more data than users realize, sharing it with advertisers or third parties without transparent consent.

In this chapter, we'll explore the different types of IoT devices, how they function, and the ways they collect and store data. We'll also delve into the risks and vulnerabilities associated with IoT devices, providing real-world examples to illustrate these challenges. Finally, we'll offer practical tips for securing your smart home and protecting your privacy in the connected age.

Understanding the privacy implications of IoT devices is essential for navigating this new frontier of technology. By learning how these devices work and taking proactive steps to secure them, you can enjoy their benefits without compromising your personal data. Let's dive into the world of IoT and uncover the hidden risks of living in a connected world.

Types of IoT Devices and Their Functions

The Internet of Things encompasses a wide range of devices, each designed to make our lives easier and more connected. From home automation systems to wearable technology, these devices collect and analyse data to provide personalized experiences. However, the variety and scope of IoT devices also mean that privacy risks are widespread and multifaceted.

One prominent example of IoT devices is smart speakers like Amazon Alexa and Google Home. These devices have revolutionized home automation by allowing users to control lighting, thermostats, and even appliances with simple voice commands. They also integrate with services like Spotify and Siri, enhancing convenience and creating a seamless user experience. However, the always-on microphones required for voice activation raise concerns about eavesdropping and unintended data collection.

Wearable technology, such as fitness trackers like Fitbit and smartwatches like the Apple Watch, represents another category of IoT devices. These devices monitor everything from steps taken and calories burned to heart rates and sleep patterns. While they offer valuable insights for health-conscious users, the personal health data they collect is highly sensitive and often shared with third-party apps or healthcare providers, creating potential privacy vulnerabilities.

Home automation systems, including smart thermostats like Nest and video doorbells like Ring, further highlight the scope of IoT devices. These gadgets allow users to control their home environment remotely and provide enhanced security through real-time video feeds. However, instances of hacked security cameras and data breaches have shown how these devices can become entry points for cybercriminals.

Even mundane household appliances, such as refrigerators and ovens, are now part of the IoT ecosystem. Smart refrigerators can track inventory, suggest recipes, and notify users about expiration dates, while connected ovens can be preheated via a mobile app. While these features add convenience, they also rely on continuous data collection to function effectively, underscoring the need for robust security measures to protect users' information.

Examples of IoT Devices

IoT devices come in many forms, including:

- Smart Speakers: Devices like Amazon Echo and Google Nest allow users to control other devices, check the weather, or stream music using voice commands.
- Wearable Technology: Fitness trackers like Fitbit and Apple Watch monitor physical activity, heart rate, and sleep patterns.
- Smart Home Devices: Thermostats, lighting systems, and security cameras automate home management and provide remote access via apps.

- Healthcare Devices: Smart medical devices, such as glucose monitors and blood pressure cuffs, help patients manage chronic conditions.
- Connected Appliances: Refrigerators, washing machines, and ovens with IoT capabilities offer features like energy monitoring and remote operation.

These devices rely on sensors and internet connectivity to function, constantly gathering data about users to improve performance and provide personalized recommendations.

How IoT Devices Collect Data

IoT devices are built to collect and process data, it's what makes them "smart." Whether it's tracking your fitness goals or adjusting the temperature in your home, these devices rely on a steady stream of information. This data enables IoT devices to learn user preferences, automate tasks, and provide tailored recommendations. For example, a smart thermostat might monitor your daily routines to adjust the temperature automatically, creating a more comfortable environment while saving energy.

However, this constant collection of data raises important questions. How much information are these devices gathering, and do users truly understand the scope of what is being recorded? Many IoT devices operate in the background, collecting data without requiring explicit input from users. Sensors, cameras, and microphones continuously track and store information, often with little transparency about how it is used.

Additionally, once data is collected, it doesn't simply remain on the device. Most IoT devices send their data to cloud servers for processing, storage, or sharing with third parties. This can include manufacturers, advertisers, or even government agencies. The sheer volume of data being transmitted creates a significant risk, as breaches or misuse can expose sensitive information to unauthorized parties.

Understanding how IoT devices gather and process data is essential for making informed decisions about their use. By recognizing the mechanisms behind data collection and the potential risks involved, users can take proactive steps to protect their privacy while still enjoying the benefits of smart technology.

Data Collection Methods

- Sensors: Most IoT devices use sensors to collect data. For example, smart thermostats measure temperature and humidity, while wearable devices track movement and heart rate.

- Voice Commands: Smart speakers like Alexa and Google Assistant record and process voice commands to fulfil user requests.
- Camera Feeds: Security cameras and doorbell cameras capture video footage that can be accessed remotely.
- App Interactions: IoT devices often require companion apps, which collect additional data, such as location and usage patterns.

Data Storage and Sharing

Once data is collected, it is typically stored on cloud servers operated by the device manufacturer. From there, it may be shared with third parties, including advertisers, analytics companies, and sometimes even government agencies. For instance, data from a fitness tracker might be shared with healthcare providers or insurers to create personalized health plans.

Risks and Vulnerabilities in Smart Homes

Smart homes are the epitome of convenience, but they come with significant risks. The interconnected nature of IoT devices means that a single vulnerability can compromise an entire system. Understanding these risks is crucial for safeguarding your home and personal data.

One of the biggest challenges with smart homes is the reliance on multiple devices connected to a single network. A weak link, such as a smart camera with outdated firmware or a device with a default password, can become an entry point for hackers. Once inside, attackers can potentially access other devices on the network, such as smart thermostats, security cameras, or even personal computers. This interconnectedness magnifies the potential damage of a single vulnerability.

Another concern is the sheer volume of data collected by smart home devices. Devices like smart speakers and security cameras constantly monitor their surroundings, capturing audio, video, and other personal information. This data is often stored in the cloud, which, while convenient, also increases the risk of breaches or unauthorized access. When combined with the possibility of manufacturers sharing data with third parties, the risks to personal privacy become even more pronounced.

Common Vulnerabilities

- Weak Passwords: Many IoT devices come with default passwords that users often forget to change, making them easy targets for hackers.

- Unsecured Networks: If your home Wi-Fi network isn't secure, it can serve as a gateway for attackers to access connected devices.
- Outdated Software: Manufacturers often fail to provide regular software updates, leaving devices vulnerable to known exploits.

Real-World Example

In 2016, a massive cyberattack known as the Mirai botnet used IoT devices with weak security to launch a distributed denial-of-service (DDoS) attack. This attack took down major websites like Twitter, Netflix, and PayPal, highlighting how unsecured devices can be weaponized.

Tips for Securing IoT Devices

While IoT devices come with inherent risks, there are steps you can take to secure them and protect your privacy. Implementing these best practices can significantly reduce your exposure to potential threats. By taking proactive measures, you can prevent common vulnerabilities from being exploited and ensure that your personal information remains private.

Ignoring the security of IoT devices can lead to serious consequences. Hackers can infiltrate poorly secured networks, gaining access to everything from smart thermostats to security cameras. Such breaches can result in stolen personal data, unauthorized surveillance, or even financial fraud. These risks underscore the importance of adopting effective security practices.

Additionally, many IoT devices collect and transmit data to cloud servers, creating another potential point of vulnerability. Without proper safeguards, sensitive data, such as video feeds or health metrics, can fall into the wrong hands. Securing your devices not only protects you but also helps create a safer environment for everyone using interconnected technology.

Best Practices

- Change Default Passwords: Always update the default password on your devices to something strong and unique.
- Enable Two-Factor Authentication (2FA): Whenever possible, enable 2FA for an added layer of security.
- Use a Separate Network: Create a dedicated Wi-Fi network for IoT devices to isolate them from your main devices.
- Keep Software Updated: Regularly check for and install firmware updates to patch security vulnerabilities.

- Disable Unnecessary Features: Turn off features like remote access or voice activation if you don't use them.
- Monitor Device Activity: Use network monitoring tools to detect unusual behaviour from your IoT devices.

By following these tips, you can enjoy the benefits of IoT technology without sacrificing your privacy.

Conclusion

IoT devices have revolutionized the way we live, offering unparalleled convenience and functionality. However, they also pose significant privacy risks that cannot be ignored. By understanding how these devices collect data and the vulnerabilities they introduce, you can take proactive steps to protect your personal information.

Securing your smart home is not just about using the latest technology, it's about adopting habits that prioritize privacy and safety. Change default passwords, update software, and monitor device activity to minimize risks. Remember, in the connected age, privacy is a choice. With the right knowledge and tools, you can enjoy the benefits of IoT without compromising your security.

Navigating Social Media Without Compromising Privacy

Social media has become an integral part of our lives, connecting us to friends, family, and communities across the globe. Platforms like Facebook, Instagram, and TikTok have redefined how we share information, stay updated on current events, and express ourselves. However, as much as social media has revolutionized communication, it has also brought with it serious privacy concerns. These platforms collect vast amounts of data, track user behaviour, and monetize our digital presence. For those unaware, social media can be a gateway to compromised privacy and potential harm.

Imagine sharing a harmless vacation photo on Instagram. Unbeknownst to you, the geotag embedded in the image reveals your exact location, and someone with ill intentions uses this information to determine that your home is unoccupied. Such scenarios are not just hypothetical; they underscore the risks of oversharing on platforms that prioritize engagement over security. While social media can be a powerful tool for connection, it is essential to understand the trade-offs and learn how to use these platforms responsibly.

The concerns about social media privacy extend beyond individual users. Governments and organizations have raised alarms about how data collected by platforms is used, especially when it involves foreign ownership. A notable example is the U.S. government's scrutiny of TikTok, citing fears that user data could be accessed by the Chinese government. This led to calls for bans and restrictions, highlighting how social media privacy is a global issue that affects individuals and nations alike.

In this chapter, we will explore how social media platforms track user behaviour, the risks of oversharing, and practical steps to enhance your privacy on popular platforms. By understanding how these platforms operate and taking proactive measures, you can continue to enjoy the benefits of social media while safeguarding your personal information.

Social media doesn't have to be a trade-off between connection and privacy. With the right tools and habits, you can navigate these platforms confidently and securely. Let's dive into the mechanics of social media tracking, the dangers of oversharing, and the steps you can take to protect yourself online.

How Social Media Platforms Track User Behaviour

When you use social media, you might think you're simply scrolling through your feed, liking posts, or sharing updates. However, every click, tap, and interaction you make is being tracked. Social media platforms are designed to collect as much information about their users as possible. This data collection isn't random; it's part of a deliberate strategy to gather insights that can be monetized through targeted advertising, content optimization, and behavioural predictions.

The motivations behind this tracking are rooted in the business models of social media companies. These platforms operate on a model where user engagement translates to revenue. By tracking your actions, platforms can deliver highly personalized content that keeps you scrolling, clicking, and engaging, increasing their ad impressions and revenue. What may seem like a harmless recommendation for a new video or friend connection is often the result of sophisticated algorithms designed to maximize your time on the platform.

Over the years, the methods of data collection have evolved significantly. Early social media platforms relied on basic metrics like post views and clicks. Today, advanced machine learning algorithms analyse everything from the tone of your comments to the duration you spend viewing specific types of content. This evolution underscores the need for users to stay informed about how their behaviour is being tracked and used, as the implications for privacy continue to grow more complex. This data is then analysed to create detailed profiles, which are used for targeted advertising and content recommendations.

Methods of Tracking

- Cookies and Tracking Pixels: Social media platforms use cookies to monitor your activity, not only on their sites but also across the web. Tracking pixels embedded in posts or ads allow these platforms to gather data about what you view, click, and interact with.

- Engagement Metrics: Every like, comment, share, and follow is logged. Platforms analyse this data to understand your preferences and predict what content will keep you engaged longer.

- Location Data: Many platforms request or track your location, either through geotagging features or by accessing GPS data from your device. For example, Instagram can use your location to suggest nearby places or events.

- Behavioural Analysis: Advanced algorithms analyse your behaviour to identify patterns. For instance, if you frequently engage with posts about fitness, the platform may assume you're interested in related topics and show you ads for workout gear or gym memberships.

Real-Life Example

A well-documented case of data tracking involves Facebook's Cambridge Analytica scandal. In 2018, it was revealed that a third-party app collected data from millions of Facebook users without their explicit consent. This data was then used for political advertising, raising significant concerns about how user information is harvested and utilized.

Risks of Oversharing: Identity Theft and Targeted Scams

Sharing personal moments on social media can feel rewarding, but oversharing can have unintended consequences. Information shared online can be exploited by bad actors for identity theft, scams, or even physical threats. The very nature of social media encourages sharing, as platforms thrive on user engagement and the continuous stream of updates. However, this societal pressure to share every detail of our lives can expose us to risks we might not fully understand.

One psychological factor driving oversharing is the need for validation. Receiving likes, comments, and shares provides a dopamine boost, making users feel valued and appreciated. This reinforcement loop encourages people to share even more, often without considering the potential consequences of revealing too much personal information. For instance, a simple post celebrating a new job could inadvertently share details about your workplace, position, or routines that bad actors could exploit.

On a societal level, the culture of connectivity further normalizes oversharing. Many people feel compelled to maintain an online presence to stay relevant or connected, leading them to post details about their personal lives, family members, and even their daily schedules. Unfortunately, this wealth of publicly available information can be a goldmine for cybercriminals, who can piece together data to target individuals with phishing scams, fraud, or other malicious activities. Understanding these dynamics is essential to making more mindful decisions about what we choose to share online.

Risks of Oversharing

Identity Theft: Sharing too much information, such as your full name, date of birth, or address, can make it easier for cybercriminals to steal your identity. They may use this information to open credit accounts, file fraudulent tax returns, or access sensitive accounts.

Targeted Scams: Scammers often use details shared on social media to craft convincing phishing attempts. For example, a scammer might learn about your recent vacation and send a fake email posing as your airline, asking for payment to confirm your booking.

Physical Security Risks: Geotagging and posting about your location in real time can alert criminals to your whereabouts. For instance, announcing that you're on vacation could signal that your home is empty.

Fictional Scenario

Consider Sarah, a 30-year-old teacher who frequently shares her life on Instagram. She posts a photo of her new driver's license to celebrate getting her first car. Excited, she forgets to blur out her full name, address, and license number. A cybercriminal sees the post and uses the information to apply for a credit card in her name. Weeks later, Sarah is shocked to find fraudulent charges on her credit report, all because of one innocent post.

Privacy Settings for Popular Platforms

Social media platforms offer privacy settings, but many users either overlook or don't fully understand them. These settings are your first line of defines against unwanted data collection and exposure. Platforms like Facebook,

Instagram, and TikTok often prioritize user engagement and data collection over clear communication about privacy tools, making it crucial for users to take the initiative in protecting their information.

User awareness is a key factor in safeguarding personal data. Many people assume their information is safe by default, without realizing the extent to which platforms track and store data. Privacy settings, when correctly configured, can significantly reduce the amount of personal information exposed to advertisers, third parties, and even potential bad actors. For example, limiting who can see your posts or disabling location tracking can go a long way in enhancing your digital safety.

However, these settings are often buried in menus or phrased in ways that make them difficult to understand. This intentional complexity can leave users vulnerable, as platforms benefit from a lack of transparency. By taking the time to understand and implement these tools, users can reclaim some control over their online presence, turning social media into a more secure space for connection and expression.

Platform-Specific Privacy Checklists

- Facebook:
  Set your profile to private so only friends can see your posts.

Turn off location sharing.

Review apps and websites connected to your account and remove those you no longer use.

Use two-factor authentication (2FA) for added security.

- Instagram:
  Make your account private so only approved followers can see your content.
  Disable geotagging for posts and stories.
  Review your follower list and remove any accounts you don't recognize.

- TikTok:
  Set your account to private, ensuring that only approved followers can view your videos.
  Disable the app's location tracking feature.
  Limit who can comment on or duet with your videos.

Real-Life Example: TikTok Ban in the USA

TikTok has faced intense scrutiny over its data practices, particularly because its parent company, ByteDance, is based in China. U.S. officials have raised concerns that user data collected by TikTok could be accessed by the Chinese government. In 2020, the Trump administration attempted to ban TikTok, citing national security risks. Although the ban was never fully implemented, it sparked a global conversation about the privacy implications of social media platforms and the need for stricter regulations.

Conclusion

Social media has become a cornerstone of modern communication, but it comes with significant privacy challenges. By understanding how these platforms track user behaviour, recognizing the risks of oversharing, and taking advantage of privacy settings, you can regain control over your digital footprint. Remember, protecting your privacy doesn't mean abandoning social media altogether, it means using it wisely and responsibly.

With proactive steps, such as configuring privacy settings, limiting the information you share, and staying vigilant about potential scams, you can enjoy the benefits of social media without compromising your security. In an era where data is power, safeguarding your personal information is more important than ever. Let's embrace social media as a tool for connection, while keeping our privacy intact.

The Future of Privacy: AI, Biometrics, and Digital Identity

As technology evolves, so do the challenges to maintaining privacy in an increasingly connected world. Artificial intelligence (AI), biometrics, and digital identity systems are at the forefront of innovation, promising to revolutionize how we interact with technology. However, these advancements also bring significant risks, raising questions about how personal data is collected, stored, and used. While new technologies offer potential solutions to privacy concerns, they also create new vulnerabilities that demand our attention.

Imagine a future where facial recognition technology is so advanced that it identifies you instantly as you walk into a store, offering personalized discounts based on your shopping history. On the surface, this might seem convenient, but beneath this efficiency lies a troubling reality: a complete loss of anonymity. In this future, every interaction could be tracked, recorded, and analysed, leaving no room for privacy. This is not science fiction; these technologies are already being implemented in various forms today.

Governments and corporations are increasingly adopting digital identity systems and biometric authentication methods to streamline services and enhance security. For instance, some countries have introduced national ID systems that combine biometric data, like fingerprints or iris scans, with personal information. While these systems can reduce fraud and improve efficiency, they also centralize sensitive data, making it a prime target for hackers and misuse.

In this chapter, we will explore the role of AI and biometrics in shaping the future of privacy, examine the risks associated with digital identity systems, and highlight promising technologies that could protect our data. By understanding these emerging trends, we can better prepare for the challenges ahead and make informed decisions about how we navigate the digital world.

The future of privacy is uncertain, but it is not without hope. Innovations like blockchain and advanced encryption techniques offer promising solutions to safeguard our data. However, balancing technological progress with the right to privacy will require collaboration between governments, corporations, and individuals. Let's dive into the technologies shaping the future and uncover how we can protect our privacy in the years to come.

Advancements in AI and Biometrics

Artificial intelligence and biometrics are transforming the way we interact with technology. AI algorithms are increasingly used to analyse vast amounts of data, while biometric systems rely on unique physical characteristics, such as fingerprints and facial features, to authenticate users. Together, these technologies promise greater convenience and security but also raise significant privacy concerns.

AI has already become a part of our daily routines, often in ways we don't realize. From personalized shopping recommendations to voice assistants like Siri and Alexa, AI systems analyse user preferences and behaviours to provide tailored services. While this enhances user experiences, it also creates detailed profiles that companies can exploit for profit, raising questions about how much personal data is too much to share.

Biometrics have similarly made their way into everyday life. Smartphones with fingerprint or facial recognition features, like Apple's Face ID, have normalized the use of biometric data for authentication. These technologies offer a level of security that passwords often cannot match, but they also carry unique risks. Unlike passwords, which can be reset, biometric data is permanent. If compromised, the consequences could be far-reaching and irreversible.

The growing reliance on AI and biometrics highlights both the potential and the perils of these technologies. On one hand, they can make life more efficient and secure. On the other, they raise critical questions about consent, transparency, and the trade-offs between convenience and privacy. As these technologies continue to evolve, understanding their impact on privacy will be essential for making informed decisions about how we interact with them.

AI in Data Analysis

AI excels at processing and analysing large datasets, making it a powerful tool for organizations that rely on user data. For example, machine learning algorithms can predict consumer behaviour, detect fraudulent activities, and optimize personalized experiences. Social media platforms use AI to curate content, while online retailers employ it to recommend products based on browsing history.

However, the use of AI in data analysis often comes at the expense of privacy. AI systems require extensive amounts of data to function effectively, and this data is often collected without users' explicit consent. Additionally, AI algorithms can inadvertently perpetuate biases if the data used to train them is not representative or ethical. This highlights the need for transparency and accountability in AI development.

Biometric Authentication

Biometric systems, such as fingerprint scanners and facial recognition software, are becoming commonplace in smartphones, airports, and even banking services. These systems offer a higher level of security compared to traditional passwords, as biometric data is unique to each individual. For instance, Apple's Face ID and fingerprint authentication are widely regarded as secure methods for accessing devices.

Despite their benefits, biometric systems pose unique risks. Unlike passwords, biometric data cannot be changed if it is compromised. A stolen fingerprint or facial scan could have long-term implications, as this data is often linked to sensitive accounts or systems. Furthermore, the storage of biometric data raises concerns about how securely this information is managed and who has access to it.

Risks of Digital Identity Systems

Digital identity systems are designed to simplify and secure online interactions by consolidating personal information into a single digital profile. While these systems have the potential to reduce fraud and improve accessibility, they also introduce significant privacy risks. Centralizing sensitive data makes these systems attractive targets for cyberattacks and misuse.

Globally, the adoption of digital identity systems is accelerating. Countries like India, Estonia, and Sweden have implemented national digital ID programs, aiming to streamline access to services ranging from banking to healthcare. These systems promise to enhance efficiency and provide greater inclusivity by offering a single point of identification for all citizens. However, this convenience comes with a cost, the centralization of personal information into databases that can become lucrative targets for hackers.

The societal implications of digital identity systems are profound. By linking various aspects of an individual's life, these systems create detailed profiles that can be used not only for service delivery but also for surveillance and control. In some regions, governments have faced criticism for leveraging digital identities to monitor citizens' activities, raising ethical questions about the balance between security and privacy.

Moreover, the risks extend beyond misuse by governments. Corporate reliance on digital identity systems for customer verification and targeted services has amplified concerns about data privacy. When companies collect and store biometric data or other personal details, they become custodians of highly sensitive information. Without robust safeguards, these systems can lead to breaches, misuse, or unintended consequences that compromise individual autonomy and privacy.

Centralization of Data

Digital identity systems often store large amounts of personal information, including biometric data, financial records, and health details, in centralized databases. This centralization creates a single point of failure. If a database is breached, the consequences can be catastrophic, exposing users to identity theft, fraud, and other forms of exploitation.

One real-world example is India's Aadhaar system, the largest biometric ID program in the world. While Aadhaar aims to streamline access to government services, it has faced criticism for its security vulnerabilities. Data breaches have exposed the personal information of millions of users, highlighting the risks of relying on centralized digital identity systems.

Surveillance and Misuse

Digital identity systems can also be exploited for surveillance purposes. Governments and corporations may use these systems to monitor citizens' activities, raising concerns about privacy and autonomy. In some cases, these systems have been used to suppress dissent or discriminate against marginalized groups, further emphasizing the need for robust safeguards and oversight.

Promising Technologies for Data Protection

As privacy concerns grow, innovative technologies are emerging to address these challenges. From blockchain to advanced encryption techniques, these tools offer new ways to protect personal data and ensure greater control over how information is shared and used. These advancements signal a shift in the way organizations and individuals think about privacy, moving from reactive solutions to proactive, user-centric approaches.

Blockchain, for instance, has garnered attention for its ability to decentralize data storage, reducing the risks associated with centralized databases. Unlike traditional systems, blockchain distributes information across multiple nodes, making it more resilient to breaches and tampering. This decentralized model not only enhances security but also empowers users to manage their own data, setting the stage for a future where privacy is no longer an afterthought but a core design principle.

Encryption technologies have also evolved significantly, providing robust solutions to protect communications and data. End-to-end encryption has become the standard for many messaging platforms, ensuring that only the intended recipients can access the content of a conversation. Meanwhile, advancements like quantum encryption are poised to revolutionize data security, leveraging the principles of quantum mechanics to create virtually unbreakable codes. These technologies promise to make hacking and data interception far more challenging for malicious actors.

As these innovations continue to develop, they hold the potential to reshape the privacy landscape, addressing many of the vulnerabilities that plague current systems. However, the adoption of these technologies is not without challenges. Widespread implementation will require collaboration among governments, businesses, and individuals, as well as a commitment to prioritizing privacy over convenience. By embracing these tools, we can take a significant step toward reclaiming control over our personal information in the digital age.

Blockchain for Data Privacy

Blockchain technology, best known for its role in cryptocurrencies, has the potential to revolutionize data protection. Unlike traditional databases, blockchain stores data in a decentralized ledger, making it more resistant to breaches and tampering. Each transaction is encrypted and verified by a network of nodes, ensuring transparency and security.

For example, blockchain can be used to create self-sovereign identities, where individuals own and control their personal information. Instead of relying on centralized databases, users can store their data in a blockchain wallet and share only the necessary details with specific parties.

This approach reduces the risk of data breaches and gives individuals greater control over their digital identities.

Advanced Encryption Techniques

Encryption is a cornerstone of data protection, and advancements in this field are making it even more effective. End-to-end encryption, for instance, ensures that data is encrypted on the sender's device and can only be decrypted by the intended recipient. This technology is widely used in messaging apps like Signal and WhatsApp to protect user communications.

Quantum encryption is another promising development. By leveraging the principles of quantum mechanics, this technology makes it virtually impossible for hackers to intercept or tamper with encrypted data. While still in its early stages, quantum encryption has the potential to set new standards for data security in the future.

Conclusion

The future of privacy is a complex landscape shaped by advancements in AI, biometrics, and digital identity systems. While these technologies offer significant benefits, they also pose new challenges that require careful consideration. By understanding the risks and exploring innovative solutions, we can navigate this evolving digital world with greater confidence and security.

Emerging technologies like blockchain and advanced encryption techniques provide hope for a more secure future, but their widespread adoption will require collaboration between governments, corporations, and individuals. As we embrace these advancements, it is crucial to prioritize privacy and ensure that technological progress does not come at the expense of our fundamental rights.

In the end, the key to protecting privacy lies in awareness, innovation, and collective action. By staying informed and advocating for stronger privacy protections, we can shape a future where technology serves us without compromising our personal freedom.

BONUS CHAPTER: The Privacy Toolkit

In today's digital age, protecting your privacy requires more than just awareness, it demands action. Fortunately, a variety of tools and resources are available to help individuals take control of their online presence. Whether you're concerned about data breaches, intrusive tracking, or securing personal communications, the right tools can make a significant difference. This chapter provides a curated list of software, apps, and actionable steps to enhance your digital privacy.

From VPNs to encrypted messaging apps, and from online privacy guides to browser security tests, this toolkit offers practical solutions for safeguarding your data. Each tool and resource has been carefully selected for its effectiveness, ease of use, and relevance to everyday digital life. By incorporating these into your routine, you can significantly reduce your vulnerability and enjoy a safer, more private online experience.

Digital privacy isn't just a personal responsibility; it's a necessity in a world where our online footprints are constantly being monitored and monetized. Hackers, corporations, and even governments often exploit digital vulnerabilities, making it more important than ever to take proactive steps. This toolkit is designed to empower you, regardless of your technical expertise, by providing accessible solutions to complex problems.

Let's explore the essential components of The Privacy Toolkit and how you can use them to protect yourself in an increasingly connected world.

Software and Apps

1. <u>Virtual Private Networks (VPNs)</u>
   VPNs are among the most effective tools for masking your IP address and encrypting your internet connection. They prevent websites, hackers, and even your internet service provider (ISP) from monitoring your online activities.

   NordVPN: Known for its speed and security, NordVPN offers features like double encryption and a strict no-logs policy. With servers in numerous countries, it allows users to bypass geographic restrictions and access content securely.

   ProtonVPN: A reliable option with a free tier, ProtonVPN emphasizes privacy and transparency, ensuring that your data remains secure. Its integration with ProtonMail enhances its credibility as a privacy-first provider.

2. Privacy Browsers
Using a privacy-focused browser can block trackers and prevent websites from collecting unnecessary data.

Brave: Blocks ads and trackers by default, offering a faster and more private browsing experience. It also includes a rewards system for users who opt to view privacy-respecting ads, providing an ethical alternative to traditional online advertising.

DuckDuckGo: A lightweight browser that prioritizes privacy and doesn't store search histories or personal information. Its search engine counterpart is also a great alternative to Google for those seeking non-tracked search results.

3. Encrypted Messaging
Secure messaging apps ensure that your conversations remain private and inaccessible to third parties.

Signal: Regarded as the gold standard for secure messaging, Signal offers end-to-end encryption for text, voice, and video communications. Its open-source nature ensures transparency and frequent audits.

Telegram: Provides encrypted messaging with features like self-destructing messages and private chat modes. While not fully end-to-end encrypted by default, its secret chat feature adds an extra layer of security.

4. Password Managers
   Managing strong, unique passwords for each account is essential for protecting your online identity.

   Bitwarden: A free, open-source password manager that stores and generates strong passwords securely. It also offers features like secure password sharing and self-hosting options for advanced users.

   Dashlane: Offers additional features like dark web monitoring and a user-friendly interface, making password management simple and effective. Its autofill functionality saves time while maintaining security.

Online Resources:

Websites Offering Privacy Education

Knowledge is power, and understanding how to protect your privacy is the first step. These websites provide valuable insights and tools:

- **EFF's Privacy Badger:** A browser extension that blocks trackers and teaches users about online privacy. Its accompanying website offers tutorials and resources on digital security.

- **Proton's Privacy Blog:** Regularly updated with tips and insights on enhancing digital security. Topics range from basic privacy practices to advanced encryption methods.

Guides for Adjusting Privacy Settings

Platforms like Facebook, Instagram, and TikTok have privacy settings that allow users to control how their data is shared. Comprehensive guides, such as those offered by the EFF or online privacy advocates, walk users through the process of configuring these settings. These guides often include screenshots and step-by-step instructions for maximum clarity.

Educational Webinars and Courses

Several organizations, such as Mozilla and the Electronic Frontier Foundation (EFF), host free webinars and courses on digital privacy. These sessions cover topics like identifying phishing scams, securing IoT devices, and using encryption tools effectively. For readers looking to deepen their understanding, these resources are invaluable.

Actionable Steps

Check for Data Breaches

Data breaches can expose sensitive information, often without the victim's knowledge. Use websites like **Have I Been Pwned** to check if your accounts have been compromised. Simply enter your email address, and the site will inform you of any known breaches involving your information. It also offers notifications for future breaches, allowing you to act quickly.

Run Browser Privacy Tests

Tools like Panopticlick by the EFF can analyse your browser's privacy settings and identify vulnerabilities. These tests highlight areas where you can improve, such as blocking trackers or disabling fingerprinting. Other tools, like Am I Unique, allow you to check if your browser's fingerprint is identifiable and take steps to anonymize your online presence.

Create a Privacy Checklist

A step-by-step checklist can help you maintain good privacy habits. Examples include:

- Regularly updating passwords and enabling 2FA.
- Reviewing app permissions on your devices.
- Clearing cookies and browser history periodically.
- Conducting monthly privacy audits to ensure your accounts remain secure.

Consider offering this checklist as a downloadable resource, allowing readers to track their progress and ensure consistent improvements. The checklist could include links to tools, guides, and additional resources for deeper engagement.

Conclusion

The Privacy Toolkit equips you with the tools and knowledge needed to protect your digital footprint. By using secure software, educating yourself with online resources, and adopting proactive habits, you can significantly enhance your privacy. Remember, digital security is not a one-time effort but an ongoing process. With the right tools and consistent effort, you can take control of your online presence and safeguard your personal information against evolving threats.

This toolkit is more than just a collection of recommendations; it's a call to action. Every small step you take to secure your digital life contributes to a broader movement toward greater privacy for all. By incorporating these tools and strategies into your daily routine, you're not just protecting yourself, you're helping to build a safer digital world for everyone.

Glossary of Terms

A

- AI (Artificial Intelligence): A branch of computer science that enables machines to perform tasks that typically require human intelligence, such as learning, decision-making, and problem-solving.
- Authentication: The process of verifying a user's identity, often using methods like passwords, biometric data, or security codes.

B

- Biometrics: Unique physical or behavioural characteristics, such as fingerprints, facial features, or voice patterns, used for identification and security purposes.
- Blockchain: A decentralized ledger technology that stores data in blocks linked chronologically, ensuring transparency and security without relying on a central authority.
- Browser Cookies: Small files stored on a user's device by websites to track browsing behaviour, save login information, and personalize user experiences.

C

- Cache: A storage location on your device that temporarily holds data to improve website and app performance.
- Centralized Data: Data stored in a single database or server, which can create a single point of failure if breached.

- Cybersecurity: Measures and practices designed to protect digital systems, networks, and data from unauthorized access or attacks.

D

- Data Breach: An incident where sensitive, protected, or confidential information is accessed, stolen, or disclosed without authorization.
- Digital Identity: An online profile that combines personal information, login credentials, and other data to represent an individual in digital spaces.
- Distributed Denial-of-Service (DDoS): A type of cyberattack that floods a server or network with traffic, causing it to crash or become unavailable.

E

- Encryption: The process of converting information into a code to prevent unauthorized access, ensuring data security during transmission or storage.
- End-to-End Encryption: A form of encryption where only the sender and recipient can read the transmitted data, with no intermediaries able to access it.

F

- Facial Recognition Technology: A biometric technology that identifies or verifies a person's identity using their facial features.
- Fingerprint Scanner: A biometric device used to identify or authenticate users by analysing their unique fingerprint patterns.

G

- GDPR (General Data Protection Regulation): A European Union regulation that protects personal data and privacy for individuals within the EU and governs data transfer outside the region.
- Geofencing: A technology that creates virtual boundaries around a geographic area, triggering specific actions when a user enters or exits that area.

I

- Internet of Things (IoT): A network of interconnected devices, such as smart home appliances and wearable tech, that collect and share data via the internet.
- IP Address: A unique string of numbers assigned to each device connected to the internet, used to identify and locate devices.

L

- Location Tracking: The process of monitoring a user's geographic location through GPS, Wi-Fi, or other technologies.

M

- Metadata: Data that provides information about other data, such as the time a message was sent or the location of a photo.
- Multi-Factor Authentication (MFA): A security method requiring two or more verification steps to authenticate a user, such as a password and a fingerprint.

P

- Phishing: A cyberattack where attackers pose as legitimate entities to trick individuals into providing sensitive information like passwords or credit card numbers.
- Predictive Algorithms: Algorithms that analyse data patterns to make predictions about future behaviour or trends, often used in AI systems.
- Privacy Settings: Options within apps or platforms that allow users to control how their personal information is collected, shared, and displayed.

Q

- Quantum Encryption: An advanced form of encryption that uses the principles of quantum mechanics to create highly secure data transmission systems.

S

- Social Engineering: Manipulative tactics used by attackers to trick individuals into divulging confidential information or granting access to systems.
- Surveillance Capitalism: An economic system where companies monetize personal data collected through digital tracking and analysis.

T

- Tracking Pixels: Invisible images embedded in emails or websites that track user behaviour, such as when an email is opened or a link is clicked.
- Two-Factor Authentication (2FA): A security method requiring two separate forms of identification, such

as a password and a verification code, to access an account.

U

- User Data: Information collected from users by apps, websites, or devices, including personal details, preferences, and browsing history.

V

- VPN (Virtual Private Network): A tool that creates a secure, encrypted connection over the internet, masking the user's IP address and location.

W

- Wearable Technology: Devices like fitness trackers and smartwatches that collect and transmit data about the user's activity, health, and location.

Z

- Zero-Trust Security: A cybersecurity model that requires verification for every user and device attempting to access a network, regardless of their location or prior access.

Authors note

Thank you for reading 'You are being watched'.

I really hope you enjoyed its content. If you have a moment, I would be grateful if you could share your thoughts in an Amazon review. Your feedback will help other readers to discover my work. Some examples below.

And I would like to take the opportunity to thank for my family and friends for being in my life, inspiring yet challenging me to improve myself every day.

Synthia